Coliola's Absolutely Amazing Alphabet

Story by Candi Werenka

Illustrations by Bethany Harris

Text copyright © 2021 by Candi Werenka, Coliola Books

Illustration's copyright © 2021 by Bethany Harris

All rights reserved. Reproduction in part or in whole is strictly forbidden without the express written consent of the publisher, except for a brief quotation for review purposes.

Postures created by Dr. Laurette Willis. PraiseMoves ® is a registered trademark of PraiseMoves Fitness Ministry, Dr. Laurette Willis, and PraiseMoves, LLC http://PraiseMoves.com.

Hebrew alphabet education derived from Hebrew Word Pictures. Copyright © 2018 by Dr. Frank T. Seekins. All rights reserved.

Scripture taken from the New King James Version ®. Copyright © 1982 by Thomas Nelson. Used by permission. All rights reserved.

Covers and interior layout by Orand Werenka

ISBN: 978-1-7776242-2-4

This book is dedicated to Christine Ross and all the wonderful PraiseMoves instructors and their families. May you continue to exemplify 1 Corinthians 6:20, and "glorify God in your bodies and in your spirits, which are God's."

Disclaimer

The author strongly recommends that you consult with your physician before beginning any exercise program. You should be in good physical condition and be able to participate in these exercises. The author is not a licensed healthcare provider and has no expertise in diagnosing, examining, or treating medical conditions of any kind, or in determining the effect of any specific exercise on a medical condition.

When participating in any exercise program, there is the possibility of physical injury. If you engage in these exercises, you agree that you do so at your own risk, are voluntarily participating, assume all risk of injury to yourself, and agree to release and discharge the author from any, and all claims or causes of action, known or unknown, arising out of the contents of this book.

The author advises you to take full responsibility for your safety and know your limits while practicing the exercises described in this book. Do not take risks beyond your level of experience, aptitude, training, and comfort level.

An Important Message for Kids and Adults

The Hebrew alphabetic postures in this book were thoughtfully created by Dr. Laurette Willis. A posturing form of exercise is important, because even though it is good to exercise our hearts, it is also good to stretch our muscles.

Stretching makes our muscles stronger physically so we will not get injured as easily when we participate in other sports. We are also getting stronger mentally and spiritually because we are learning the Hebrew alphabet and coordinating Bible verses.

God created everyone special, so it is important to ask your doctor if this type of exercise is right for you. It is also important to follow directions and not push your body too hard. If you do these exercises three to five times every week, you may notice that you can stretch a little further and are less wobbly on your feet. Coliola's advice is to take it slow, drink plenty of water, and have a blast!

Coliola is a floppy-eared, black labrador and golden retriever puppy. She lives with her human family in Calgary, Alberta. She has a lot of fun adventures, just like the one she is going to take you on today.

Coliola and her friends, Tia and Mary, are going to teach you the Hebrew alphabet. Every letter in the Hebrew alphabet has a sound, just like the letters in our alphabet. The neat thing is that every letter has a picture to go along with it. These pictures were used to help write many of the letters in the world today, so they are extra special letters to learn!

Coliola, Tia, and Mary are also going to teach you an alphabetic posture and Bible verse that go along with each letter. So, grab your exercise mats and water bottles, and prepare to get stronger physically, mentally, and spiritually!

1
Alef

Who: Coliola's friend Tia is excited to show you the posture for the first letter. It is called **Alef**.

How: Kneel on your mat. Put your hands beneath your shoulders. Take a big breath in, and as you let it out, lift your right leg up so that it is in a straight line with your body. Bend your right knee. Bend your right foot. Keep your belly tight. Smile!

Hold and Say: "God brings them out of Egypt; He has strength like a wild ox." Numbers 23:22

Remember to repeat on your left side.

What: **Alef** means *ox*.

Where and When: Long ago, these big animals were used to pull carts and plow fields. Coliola and Mary think Tia looks strong like an ox after doing this posture.

Why: The Bible verse compares God's strength to the strength of an ox. It looks like this ox is ready for a drink of water!

2
Bet

Who: It is Mary's turn. She is going to show you the posture for the second letter. It is called **Bet**.

How: Sit on your mat with your legs together and feet flexed. Take a big breath in, and as you let it out, tighten your belly and lean forward. Stretch your arms out straight in front of you. Keep your fingertips up and your palms forward, like you are pressing them against a wall. Smile!

Hold and Say: "How lovely is your tabernacle, O Lord of Hosts!"
Psalm 84:1

What: **Bet** means *home*.

Where and When: Long ago, tents were used by some people as homes. Coliola and Tia sleep in tents when they are camping, but they are thankful for their homes!

Why: Did you know that the word tabernacle means *meeting place*? In the Bible, it was a place where people met with God, so it was kind of like God's home.

3
Gimmel

Who: Tia is ready to show you the posture for the third letter. It is called **Gimmel**.

How: Kneel on your mat. Take a big breath in, and as you let it out, put your right foot on the mat in front of you. Bend your right knee. Interlock your thumbs and raise your arms over your head. Make sure your knee is above your ankle and your shoulders are down and back. Look up and smile!

Hold and Say: "For it is easier for a camel to go through the eye of a needle than for a rich man to enter the kingdom of God."
Luke 18:25

Remember to repeat on your left side.

What: **Gimmel** means *camel*.

Where and When: *A group of camels travelling together* is called a caravan. Coliola and Mary think camels are cool, but they are puzzled about the eye of the needle in the Bible verse.

Why: The eye of the needle is *the hole at the top of a needle where the thread goes through.* It is important not to put material things before what pleases God.

4
Dalet

Who: The fourth letter is called **Dalet**. Mary is over the moon to show you the posture.

How: Stand straight. Inhale, and as you exhale, reach your right arm out to the side with your palm facing down. Bring your left arm behind your back and place the back of your hand as close to your right shoulder as possible. Next, reach your right outstretched arm up and bend it at the elbow. Can you touch your fingers? A belt will help. Smile!

Hold and Say: "Behold, I stand at the door and knock. If anyone hears My voice and opens the door, I will come into him and dine with him, and he with Me."
Revelation 3:20

Remember to repeat on your left side.

What: **Dalet** means *door*.

Where and When: Long ago, some people used animal hides as doors to their homes.

Why: Coliola and Tia think their lives are like doors. The Bible verse tells us that God stands at the door to our lives and knocks, and it is our choice to let Him come in.

5
Hey

Who: **Hey** is the fifth letter. Tia says, "Hey, hey, hey, are you ready to join in?"

How: Stand with your feet wide apart, your toes pointed out, and your knees bent over your ankles. Take a big breath in, and as you let it out, raise your arms with your palms up. Keep your legs pressed back, your body straight, and your tailbone tucked in to protect your back. Tighten your belly. Smile!

Hold and Say: "Then Mary said, 'Behold the maidservant of the Lord! Let it be to me according to your word.' And the angel departed from her."
Luke 1:38

What: **Hey** means *behold*.

Where and When: Behold means *to look at something with amazement*. Long ago, people would sometimes raise their arms in excitement when they used this letter.

Why: The girl named Mary in the Bible accepted what God wanted for her life without complaining. Next time you feel like complaining, behold Mary and her good attitude.

Time for a water break!

6
Vav

Who: The sixth letter is called **Vav**. Mary is raring to go with the posture for this letter.

How: Stand straight. Take a big breath in, and as you let it out, raise your arms forward. Bring your palms together and interlock your fingers. You can release your pointer fingers and cross one thumb over the other. Look up past your hands. Press your elbows together. Keep your belly tight. Smile!

Hold and Say: "The words of the wise are like goads, and the words of scholars are like well-driven nails, given by one Shepherd."
Ecclesiastes 12:11

What: **Vav** means *nail*.

Where and When: Coliola and Tia are puzzled. What do you think the word goad means in the Bible verse?

Why: Goad means *to guide*. Shepherds once used long sticks called staffs to help guide their sheep to safety or new pastures. Jesus is known as the Good Shepherd in the Bible.

7
Zayin

Who: **Zayin** is the seventh letter. Are you ready to try the fun posture with Tia?

How: Stand straight. Take a big breath in, and as you let it out, raise your arms out to your sides with your palms down. Bring your right fingertips to touch your left shoulder. Raise your right elbow up and turn your head to the left. Smile!

Hold and Say: "'No weapon formed against you shall prosper, and every tongue which rises against you in judgement you shall condemn. This is the heritage of the servants of the Lord, and their righteousness is from Me,' says the Lord."
Isaiah 54:17

Remember to repeat on the left side.

What: **Zayin** means *weapon or sword*.

Where and When: Long ago, people made axes for tools and swords for weapons to protect themselves.

Why: Coliola and Mary think it is cool that Bible verses can be used as tools. When they feel sad or afraid, there are verses to make them feel better.

8
Chet

Who: The eighth letter is called **Chet**. It is Mary's turn to show you the back-strengthening posture.

How: Sit on your mat. Take a big breath in, and as you let it out, bend your knees. Move your arms behind you with your palms on your mat. Your fingertips should point toward the back of your feet. Push your body up and straight across, like a fence. Keep your head in line with your back. Look up and smile!

Hold and Say: "And he said: 'The Lord is my rock and my fortress and my deliverer.'"
2 Samuel 22:2

What: **Chet** means *fence*.

Where and When: Long ago, people used fences to keep their animals safe. Fences are also used this way today.

Why: A fence is like the fortress mentioned in the Bible verse. Both are used for protection, just like God protects us.

9
Tet

Who: Tia is going to show you how to do the posture for the ninth letter. It is called **Tet**.

How: Sit on your mat with your legs together and toes pointed. Take a big breath in, and as you let it out, lift your legs up. Reach your arms out in front of you with your palms facing down. Try to balance on your tailbone. Can you hold onto the outsides of your feet? Smile!

Hold and Say: "For You, O Lord, will bless the righteous; with favor You will surround him as with a shield."
Psalm 5:12

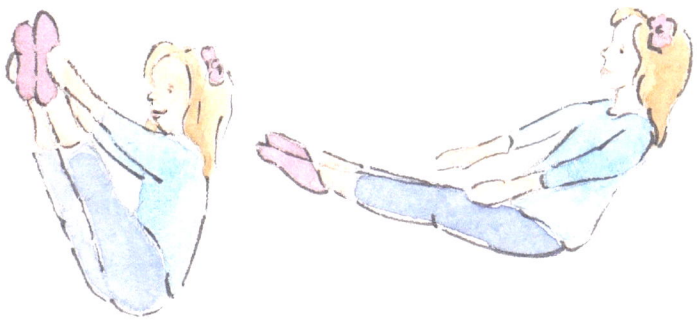

What: **Tet** means *surround*.

Where and When: A picture of something twisted or a picture of a snake were often used for the letter **Tet**.

Why: Long ago, people used shields to surround and protect themselves in battle, just like God surrounds and protects us.

10
Yod

Who: Mary is going to show you the posture for the tenth and smallest letter. It is called **Yod.**

How: Sit on your mat. Take a big breath in, and as you let it out, bring your knees to your chest. Bring your head to your knees. Wrap your arms around your knees and hold onto your wrists. Can you balance on your tailbone? Smile!

Hold and Say: "He who has a slack hand becomes poor, but the hand of the diligent makes rich."
Proverbs 10:4

What: **Yod** means *closed hand*.

Where and When: In the Torah, the letter **Yod** is used for the tenth commandment. Coliola and Tia are puzzled. What is the Torah?

Why: The Torah contains the first five books of the Bible. Did you know that the Ten Commandments are found in these first five books?

Time for a water break!

11
Kaf

Who: It is Tia's turn. She is going to show you the posture for the eleventh letter. It is called **Kaf**.

How Sit on your mat with your legs together and your toes pointed. Take a big breath in, and as you let it out, lean forward. Reach your arms straight out. Keep your palms up. Smile!

Hold and Say: "She extends her hand to the poor, yes, she reaches out her hands to the needy."
Proverbs 31:20

What: **Kaf** means *open hand*.

Where and When: A picture of the palm of a hand or the wing of a bird were often used for this letter.

Why: Can you think of ways Coliola and Mary can open their hands to those in need in their homes and communities?

12
Lamed

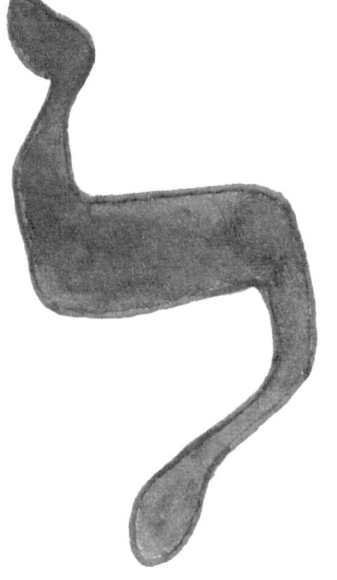

Who: The twelfth letter is called **Lamed**. Mary can hardly wait to show you the cool balancing posture.

How: Stand straight. Take a big breath in, and as you let it out, place your weight on your left leg. Place your right foot on your left foot, calf, or thigh, but not on your knee. Press your right knee back. It helps to find a point to stare at for balance. Raise your left arm up. Your palm should face forward. Place your right arm behind your head and hold your left elbow. Smile!

Hold and Say: "Death and life are in the power of the tongue, and those who love it will eat its fruit."
Proverbs 18:21

Remember to repeat on the left side.

What: **Lamed** means *tongue*.

Where and When: Long ago, shepherds guided their sheep with long sticks called staffs. A picture of a shepherd's staff is often used for the letter **Lamed**.

Why: Coliola and Tia are surprised that something as small as the tongue is so powerful. They want to be careful not to hurt others with their words.

13
Mem

Who: The thirteenth letter is called **Mem**. Tia is all set to show you the shoulder-strengthening posture.

How: Kneel on your mat. Take a big breath in, and as you let it out, put your hands on the mat behind you. Your fingers should point toward your toes. Lift your hips up. Keep your belly tight. Look up and smile!

Hold and Say: "He makes me to lie down in green pastures; He leads me beside the still waters."
Psalm 23:2

What: **Mem** means *water*.

Where and When: Water is just as important today as it was long ago. We all need water to live, be healthy, and grow.

Why: Coliola and Mary make sure they drink eight to ten glasses of water every day to keep their bodies healthy. Did you know that the Bible is like water? It helps us grow spiritually when we spend time reading it.

14
Nun

Who: **Nun** is the fourteenth letter. Are you ready to do the posture with Mary?

How: Sit on your mat with your legs straight out in front of you. Take a big breath in, and as you let it out, bring the bottoms of your feet together. Keep your feet tucked in and hold onto your ankles. Press your elbows into your knees and gently try to lower them to your mat. Sit up straight. Smile!

Hold and Say: "If a son asks for bread from any father among you, will he give him a stone? Or if he asks for a fish, will he give him a serpent instead of a fish?" Luke 11:11

What: **Nun** means *fish darting through water*. **Nun** is pronounced like the word noon.

Where and When: When a picture of a darting fish was used in the Hebrew language, it meant action or life.

Why: Coliola and Tia like giving and receiving gifts. They would rather get a fish as a gift instead of a stone, but they think the best gift they could ever get is having a friend like Jesus.

15
Samech

Who: The fifteenth letter is called **Samech**. Tia would like you to lie down in prone position for this posture. Prone means *lying on your belly*.

How: Lie on your belly with your forehead on your mat. Place your arms at your sides with your palms up. Take a big breath in, and as you let it out, raise your head, arms, and legs all at once. Keep your lower body tight to protect your back. Look up and smile!

Hold and Say: "They confronted me in the day of my calamity, but the Lord was my support."
Psalm 18:18

What: **Samech** means *support*.

Where and When: Support means *to help or hold something up*. When Coliola and Mary help their families with gardening, they sometimes use strong sticks to support young plants and trees.

Why: Coliola and Mary think their families are like strong sticks, because they give them support. That must make God the strongest stick of all!

Time for a water break!

16
Ayin

Who: The sixteenth letter is called **Ayin**. Mary would like you to be seated to do the posture.

How: Sit on your mat with your legs straight out in front of you. Make sure your back is straight and your belly is tight. Take a big breath in, and as you let it out, lift your right arm and right leg straight out. Keep your palm down and your toes pointed. Make sure your belly is tight. Smile!

Hold and Say: "But as it is written: 'Eye has not seen, nor ear heard, nor have entered into the heart of man the things which God has prepared for those who love Him.'"
1 Corinthians 2:9

Remember to repeat on the left side.

FOCUSED
DOCTORS OF OPTOMETRY

What: **Ayin** means *eye*.

Where and When: Many languages use a picture of an eye to mean *seeing or understanding*, like the Chinese word mù.

Why: Coliola and Tia thank God for their eyes. They make sure they visit their eye doctor for checkups and keep their eyes healthy by eating fruits and vegetables.

17
Pe

Who: The seventeenth letter is called **Pe**. Are you ready to join Tia for the posture?

How: Kneel on your mat. Place your hands on your hips with your fingertips facing forward. Take a big breath in, and as you let it out, slowly lean back. You can look forward or up. Smile!

Hold and Say: "Let the words of my mouth and the meditation of my heart be acceptable in Your sight, O Lord, my Strength and my Redeemer."
Psalm 19:14

What: **Pe** means *mouth*.

Where and When: The letter **Pe** also stands for the number 80. The Bible tells us that Moses was 80 years old when he led the Hebrew people out of Egypt.

Why: Did you know that the things we think about, we sometimes end up saying? It is important to think good things, so we say good things.

18
Tsadde

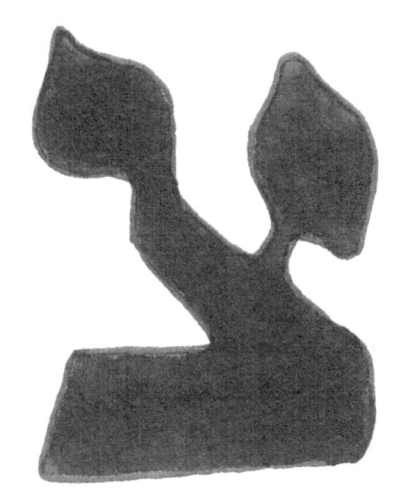

Who: Mary wonders if you are ready to do the posture for the eighteenth letter. It is called **Tsadde**.

How: Sit on your mat with your legs together and toes pointed. Take a big breath in, and as you let it out, reach your arms out with your palms up. Lean back gently. Smile!

Hold and Say: "Nevertheless, lest we offend them, go to the sea, cast in a hook, and take the fish that comes up first. And when you have opened its mouth, you will find a piece of money; take that and give it to them for Me and you."
Matthew 17:27

What: **Tsadde** means *fishhook*.

Where and When: **Tsadde** is pronounced like the zz in pizza. Coliola and Tia love pizza, but they are puzzled. What does a fishhook have to do with pizza?

Why: A fishook has nothing to do with pizza, but we should be careful about the things we get "hooked" on. If we eat too much pizza instead of doing our alphabetic postures, that may not be a good thing!

19
Kuf

Who: The nineteenth letter is called **Kuf**. Tia is ready to show you the posture.

How: Stand straight. Take a big breath in, and as you let it out, bend forward. Round your back and put your hands on your legs above your knees. Your fingers should be pointing toward each other. Push your elbows down. Keep your knees soft and your belly tucked. Smile!

Hold and Say: "You have hedged me behind and before and laid Your hand upon me."
Psalm 139:5

What: **Kuf** means *back of the head*.

Where and When: Did you know that the letter **Kuf** is also used for the number 100?

Why: Coliola and Mary know that God made their entire bodies, from the fronts and backs of their heads to the tops and bottoms of their feet.

20
Resh

Who: **Resh** is the twentieth letter. Mary reminds you to try your best with the posture.

How: Stand straight with your feet together. Take a big breath in, and as you let it out, raise your arms overhead. Your palms should face each other. Gently bend to the right. Keep your belly tight to protect your back. Reach up and out. You can hold your left wrist with your right hand. Smile!

Hold and Say: "But I want you to know that the head of every man is Christ, the head of woman is man, and the head of Christ is God."
1 Corinthians 11:3

Remember to repeat on the left side.

What: **Resh** means *head*.

Where and When: Head can also mean *the source of something*. Coliola and Tia are puzzled. What does source mean?

Why: The head of a river is the source of a river because this is *where it comes from*. God created the first woman from a rib of the first man. This is what the Bible verse means when it says the head or source of a woman is man.

Time for a water break!

21
Shin

Who: The twenty-first letter is called **Shin**. This is the last posture Tia will be sharing with you. Try your best!

How: Sit on your mat with your legs spread apart. Take a big breath in, and as you let it out, slowly walk your hands along the mat in front of you. When you reach your best stretch, relax your head. Smile!

Hold and Say: "Blessed be the Lord, who has not given us as a prey to their teeth."
Psalm 124:6

What: **Shin** means *teeth*.

Where and When: The letter **Shin** is also used for the number 300. Do you know that God used Gideon and only 300 men to win a battle against a Midianite army of 120,000?

Why: Coliola takes good care of her teeth by eating dental sticks every day. Mary brushes and flosses her teeth and visits her dentist for checkups. How do you take care of your teeth?

22

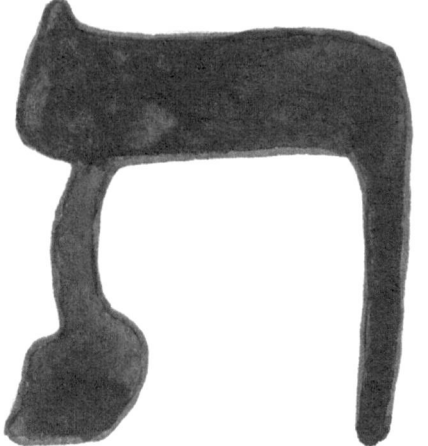

Tav

Who: The twenty-second and last letter is called **Tav**. Mary is super excited to show you Coliola's favorite posture!

How: Begin in a push-up position. Take a big breath in, and as you let it out, turn your body to the right side. Stack one foot on top of the other or leave your right knee on your mat for support. The insides of your feet should be touching if they are stacked. When you are ready, lift your left arm up. Your palm should be facing forward. Smile!

Hold and Say: "When He had called the people to Himself, with His disciples also, He said to them, 'Whoever desires to come after Me, let him deny himself, and take up his cross, and follow Me.'" Mark 8:34

Remember to repeat on the left side.

What: **Tav** means *sign* or *cross*.

Where and When: The picture of a cross has been used by many people around the world since the beginning of all languages. Coliola, Tia, and Mary all want to know why this is such an important letter.

Why: God loved us so much that He sent His only Son Jesus to die on a cross. Jesus promises to always be with us if we believe in Him and choose to follow Him by inviting Him into our hearts and lives. Coliola, Tia, and Mary have asked Jesus to be their best friend. Have you?

"For you were bought at a price; therefore glorify God in your body and in your spirit, which are God's."
1 Corinthians 6:20

Acknowledgements

A big thank you to Dr. Laurette Willis and Dr. Frank Seekins, whose perseverance and diligence have brought the Hebrew alphabetic postures and Hebrew word pictures into the mainstream. Visit www.praisemoves.com and www.livingwordpictures.com for more information.

I am thrilled with my editor, PraiseMoves instructor Jan Kamp. Jan serves as communications director for the Oaks Ministry, www.oxfordoaksministry.com, a Christ-centered residential program that offers a fresh start for women in transition. She has three sons and eight grandchildren. Jan and her husband, Ken, live in Lancaster County, PA.

I am blessed by my son, Orand Werenka, who graciously devoted his time and talents to the formatting, design, and completion of this book. Inquiries of Orand can be made at owerenka@outlook.com.

I am grateful to Hoon Kim, an innovative photographer from Calgary, Alberta. His design agency, Clarity Visual Company, offers web design, photography, videography, graphic design, and other visual arts services. Connect with Hoon at hoonkim@clarityvisual.com.

My love and appreciation to my husband Brad, sons Oakley, Orand, and Olson, and canine daughter Coliola for their support and inspiration.

Author and PraiseMoves instructor, Candi Werenka (BS, Northern Michigan University) lives in Calgary, Alberta with her husband and former NHL defenceman Brad Werenka, three sons Oakley, Orand, and Olson, and canine daughter Coliola. She enjoys homesteading, hiking, and PraiseMoves, the Christian alternative to yoga. Candi loves making others happy with homemade cards, nutritious canned goods from her garden, and educational stories for children. This is her second book in the *Tails of Coliola* series.

Illustrator Bethany Harris' (BA, University of Waterloo) paintings have received numerous awards locally and nationally. Bethany's love for God and His creation are at the heart of her energetic and captivating illustrations. She lives on a small farm in southern Alberta, where she paints, raises a flock of wooly sheep, gardens, and hikes with her dogs.

PraiseMoves instructor Christine Ross and her two daughters, Tia and Mary.

Manufactured by Amazon.ca
Bolton, ON